OUR WORLD IS RELATIVE

Julia Sooy ✶ Illustrated by Molly Walsh

Feiwel and Friends • New York

A FEIWEL AND FRIENDS BOOK

An imprint of Macmillan Publishing Group, LLC

120 Broadway, 25th floor, New York, NY 10271

Our books may be purchased in bulk for promotional, educational, or business use. Please contact your local bookseller or the Macmillan Corporate and Premium Sales Department at (800) 221-7945 ext. 5442 or by email at MacmillanSpecialMarkets@macmillan.com.

Library of Congress Cataloging-in-Publication Data

Names: Sooy, Julia, author. | Walsh, Molly (Illustrator), illustrator.

Title: Our world is relative / Julia Sooy ; illustrated by Molly Walsh.

Description: New York : Feiwel and Friends, [2019] | Summary: "A fun and engaging picture book explaining Einstein's theory of relativity."— Provided by publisher.

Identifiers: LCCN 2018039153 | ISBN 9781250293688 (hardcover)

Subjects: LCSH: General relativity (Physics)—Juvenile literature. Relativity (Physics)—Juvenile literature.

Classification: LCC QC173.6 .S6685 2019 | DDC 530.11—dc23

LC record available at https://lccn.loc.gov/2018039153

Book design by Rebecca Syracuse

Feiwel and Friends logo designed by Filomena Tuosto

First edition, 2019

The illustrations for this book were created digitally.

1 3 5 7 9 10 8 6 4 2

mackids.com

For all my many different teachers
and the worlds you've opened up
J.S.

To Nathan, Leah, and my family, who have
expanded my world in so many ways.
M.W.

Something that seems big . . .

26 inches

1 inch

... can also seem small.

It can seem like it's
not moving at all . . .

. . . and be moving very fast, too.

It can be moving forward . . .

. . . or backward, depending
on how you look at it.

A few steps . . .

. . . can be just a few feet . . .

. . . or they can take you tens of thousands of miles.

We can't see it, but light is moving.

And in the near emptiness of outer space, light moves at a constant speed.

← 299,792,458 m/s

Size, speed, weight, direction, distance—we think of space and time as fixed and measurable.

But these measurements—our experience of space and time— are relative.

Our world
is relative.

What is big? What is small?

What is moving? What is not?

What is fast? What is slow?

It can seem like we live in a world where
things are what they are.

Right is right
and left is left.

A ruler is
twelve inches.

A minute is
sixty seconds.

A ruler moving through
deep space is shorter.

My right can be your left.
Your right can be my left.

A clock moving in deep
space ticks more slowly.

But our world is relative: almost everything
exists in relation to something else.

Albert Einstein (1879–1955) was a genius. A great thinker and a brilliant physicist, he developed his famous theory of relativity in the early 1900s. This theory continues to be important to our understanding of our world and the way we experience space and time.

RESOURCES

Munroe, Randall. "The Space Doctor's Big Idea." *The New Yorker.* November 18, 2015. <www.newyorker.com/tech/elements/the-space-doctors-big-idea-einstein-general-relativity>

Einstein Online. Max Planck Institute for Gravitational Physics (Albert Einstein Institute). <www.einstein-online.info/elementary.html>